This is Alex.

Are you like Alex – a worked to the bone business owner or self-employed person?

Alex feels like she is constantly 'spinning plates' but never quite reaching her true potential, personally or professionally.

'In Cahoots': this book, the programme, the Facebook group and all of its activities have been designed to put some 'meat' on your bones.

As someone just like you, I know the demands of being a small business owner.

It is so hard to balance the demands of a business and a personal life and still feel like you are moving on, achieving growth and sustaining your business.

'In Cahoots' is a way of achieving all of these things and finding balance and success, whilst still striving for and succeeding in reaching your business and personal goals and targets.

The 'In Cahoots' book and process will give you the tools and the knowledge to do just this.

Let's find your balance, achieve growth and most importantly, reach both your and your business's true potential.

Come be 'In Cahoots' with me.

Phil

Thank You

So many people have been instrumental in the writing of this book. I have not only used my own examples, but have used many examples from the businesses I have worked with over the years and I very much would like to thank all of them.

I am very lucky in my life to be surrounded and to have always been surrounded by a barrage of strong and formidable women.

My mum, Joan, who taught me the value of hard work and that whatever life throws at you, you get up and carry on. She is inspirational.

My Grandma, Lillian Bellamy, who was and is the biggest single influence on my life. A rock, a shoulder to cry on and one of the funniest and most fun people you could ever ask to meet. She taught me the value of not having your eggs in one basket (my best business lesson ever) and the value of a song, whenever you feel scared, nervous or in need of a quick pick me up.

My Wife, Anne Teasdale. My constant source of support and the foundation on which I build everything. Ever supportive of any mad scheme I come up with and not only that an inspirational mother to our two girls and the glue that holds us all together.

My two girls, Phoebe and Madeleine. The two most precious things in my life, the funniest, maddest and most inspiring people you could ever hope to meet. Each day, no matter what my mood, they help me to raise a smile and know why I do the things I do. I just adore them.

Over the course of the last few years I have been working closely with Babson College in Boston. If you get the opportunity you should visit there, because you will leave a different and a better person. I know I did.

Two people from the many I would like to mention are the awe-inspiring Heidi Neck; I hope to be as good a teacher as she is one day. The other is the incorrigible Les Charm – to know Les is to know greatness.

Two amazing business partners Cathy Rutherford and Andrea Clarke, words cannot say how much I love being in business with these two and how many laughs we have each and every day, even when the chips are down.

Finally

Nick Wetherell, the unsung hero in this book. The designer of the cover and all of the graphics that are inside. He has the wonderful knack of being able to interpret my many ideas into a graphical form in the way I imagined them. This book would only be half as good without his input.

And finally Josie Dunne, without whom this book would have never have made it into print and you would all be watching me play the ukulele, which is a fate worth than death. Thank you Josie for kicking my butt.

The Chapters

Chapter One
What is 'In Cahoots'?

I'm Phil Teasdale, author of 'In Cahoots'.

After procrastinating for what feels like forever I decided to finally sit and write this book after 20 years of working with around 5,000 business owners and people who are running small businesses.

All of us shared a common theme and ambition: we want to grow our businesses and need techniques, tips and strategies to get to that point.

We also need support, help and perhaps most importantly a feeling that we can achieve the things we have set out to do.

When I wrote the first draft of this book, it was a very different time in the world. We hadn't heard of that word Covid and our world moved merrily along in a linear and almost placid manner.

Covid changed everything for us all in business. Not only did it have negative consequences, with people losing their routes to market and losing customers overnight, it presented us with new opportunities that we might have not thought of or even made the most of before.

After all, why would we? We know how the world works.

The 'In Cahoots' book and the programme is based around techniques that will not only help you grow your business; it will help your business to survive and thrive.

I can guarantee that this will happen to you, too, if you follow any of these techniques, because sitting down and implementing them into your business will make a difference.

I've tested it in my own business, but most importantly I've tested it with other business owners to great success.

How to use this Book

How to use this book – "is he mad?" I can hear you saying.

Does he think I don't know how to read.

Sorry, that's not what I mean at all. I know most with most books the author asks you to start at the beginning and read each chapter in a linear sequence.

That's not what I need you to do. You can if you want to, it won't hurt and you might get lots from it.

But if you are running a business like me, sometimes, I get it, you skip.

Skip to the juicy stuff, to the stuff you think is going to help you most.

So with this in mind to help you achieve your goals, read the book, but not necessarily in order.

Move to whichever chapter interests you the most and start there. Just make sure you take the tip provided and implement it into your business.

That's the key to this book, don't just read it, as lovely as it is. Implement the lessons. That's what will make the difference.

It is a lovely book, I've worked really hard on it and I hope you like it – I loved writing it!

But it's no good if you don't take the advice within it and apply it to your business.

That's how the book has been designed. Read the chapter and the implement the lesson.

Go and get a pen now – write on the book, make notes, make it relevant to you and your business. Carry it around, write over my writing if you have to, but just make sure you implement everything I am going to teach you.

Why I Wrote the Book

I came to this after my years of experience of helping business owners, which led to me learning lots of new things for my own company from the people I worked with. Some of them became mentors and then friends, and I've watched them grow and develop.

Sometimes I've watched with envy, when my business hasn't gone quite as well as theirs, but often in wonder, when I've looked at their messages and the things they've learned and implemented in their businesses, and honed and developed those new skills over the years.

Who the hell is this Phil Teasdale and what makes him qualified to give me this advice?

"I've looked him up and I've done a search and he's not a multi-millionaire, he's not well known and his businesses look good, but they are distinctly average – so why should I take advice from him?"

And here is my answer, both of these things are the truth.

I am not a multi-millionaire

My businesses are distinctly average million-pound turnover businesses.

And yet I think I am probably the most qualified person in the world to give you this advice and here's why.

I won't lie to you. I won't try and sell you a story, based on a romanticised version of what it is like to start and run a business and most importantly, my experience working with others at the ground level upwards makes me uniquely placed to give advice from a realistic view point.

Here's the other thing: implement one of these lessons into your business to see the difference it makes and if it doesn't – stop reading and believe I'm just another of those business gurus looking to make money from those saps silly enough to buy a book.

Here is the other thing – I am not going to make you get rich quick. By reading this book, your business will not become the biggest in the world overnight and most importantly I will not teach you how to get the best work life balance. I can't because I don't have these things either.

What I can do is teach you some lessons that will get you much closer to these things than you are at the moment and then I'll expect to watch you and learn from you as you own the multi-million-pound company and get the perfect work life balance.

Who am I

So this is my story. Unvarnished, and in all of its rawness.

I am a failed employee.

I can't take orders.

I have about a million ideas a day

I'm rubbish at detail

I have to be self-employed and running a business. I'm the only employer that will have me.

When I was twenty two, someone gave me some advice that I have never deviated from since.

Let me set the scene.

I had just got my first job, a recruitment job. After leaving university, I had interviewed for more than 40 and I got this one.

As someone from the North, living in London, I was used to working three jobs to pay my rent, but this was it my first proper job.

When they offered me the job, I literally skipped over London Bridge on my way to get the train home. In my suit dressed to the nines, punching the air and smiling fit to burst.

Exciting eh.

Roll forward to my first day, I was assigned a mentor, Helen.

She didn't look like all of the others in the office. It was a city based company, they all wore suits, were well coiffed and spoke with a cut glass accent.

Helen, well (I'm just going to say this 'I love Helen, she changed my life and I wouldn't but the person I am today without her), well Helen didn't look like the others. She looked a bit scruffy. She had dripped her porridge down her black jacket. She was a bit dishevelled and she had an accent that I can't quite describe.

'Come with me' she said. Off to my first client meeting I thought and here we go.

No.

Helen took me to a small café. 'This is the most important place in the whole square mile' she said. "They make the world's best salt beef sandwiches and I'll treat you to one for lunch."

We sat down, it was unusual in that it was 9.15 and she was already treating me to lunch.

I could see Helen checking me out. I prattled on, "I've never had a salt beef sandwich before".

"Perfect,"

She said, looking at me with a renewed keenness.

"I am going to give you some advice."

I was nervous. Had she worked out that my accountancy experience, which I'd used to get a foot in the door, was actually a lie?

"This is the worst company you are ever going to work for" she said. 'It really is terrible. I am only going to stay here for a year and then I'm off to Hong Kong and you are not allowed to be here past that time."

"I'm going to teach you everything I know and introduce you to everyone I know and then after twelve months, you are going to leave and set up your own desk."

And she was right, it was the worst company in the world and she did teach me everything she knew and I flew.

I developed a £1m desk for this company, 12 months passed, Helen went to Hong Kong; I set up my own desk and the terrible company sued me.

They didn't win, but it taught me that I never wanted to be employed by a terrible company again.

Ever since that moment, I have been the master of my own destiny. Sometimes getting through by the seat of my pants.

But never again for a terrible company.

Here is the thing I have learned: I like to be in control, I like the ability to make my own choices and I like to be the overriding influence.

In any business I have had or worked with since that time, I always ask the people I am working with, "Do you like to be in control?"

If the answer is yes, we work together and if the answer is no, many still succeed, they just have me to mentor them.

Why You Need a Business Mentor

Helen was my first mentor. I have so many since, funnily enough lots of them have all shared the same name, just different spellings.

Helen first
Then Geoff
Then Jeff
Then Martin
Then Heidi
And to bring it up to date Les.

I'm not too proud to say I need a mentor. It helps me to talk through ideas, it helps me to share with an impartial person and most of all it helps me personally if I am a little scared of that person and I feel like I have to please them.

I believe it's really important to find yourself a mentor when you're looking at growth and sustainment along with development and this book is intended to be your first step towards that.

After you've read it, go out and find yourself a mentor.

It could be somebody who's in business, someone you know already in your family or friend network, or somebody you admire. Whoever they are, they can become your mentor.

The Three Month Rule

You should implement a three-month rule.

You are only allowed to keep them as your direct mentor for three months, because every 12 weeks you'll have moved on in your business and in your approach.

You need to replace them with another mentor, which is not as terrible as it sounds!

Keep in contact with them of course, but when you're planning the next part of your business growth journey, you need a relevant mentor for that as well.

They can become your friends and still help, but as for the mentor, a new one every three months.

What am I trying to Achieve with 'In Cahoots'?

I want you to achieve growth within your business, but most importantly, I want you to achieve personal growth.

I want you to feel satisfied, and be honest with yourself – ask, 'Was starting this business the best thing I ever did?' And answer with a resounding yes.

I can guarantee that if you follow our programme over all of the steps, tips and tricks, you will get more from your business.

You'll grow it, but most importantly, as a business owner you will grow and develop as well.

Thank you so much for taking the time to buy and read the book. I've truly loved writing it, and there's been a lot of time, effort and consideration, not just from me, but from other business owners as well, to develop the tips and tricks shared within it.

Please take the time to implement them into your business, and thanks so much for being here and taking this time to work on your own journey to business success.

Chapter Two
Life Audit

A 'life audit' is something people often tend to do at the beginning of a new year or after their summer holiday when they don't want to go back to work.

But a life audit is really important from a business point of view, because it is really hard to be in business, and nobody tells you how difficult it is. Knowing where you are in life and being able to fully and consistently 'put a number on it" can really help you in the decision making process.

We often hear stories about people being successful in business and how wonderful self-employment is, but actually that's not true all of the time. Some days are the best days ever, but others are not just hard, they are mind-numbingly, boringly hard that it sometimes makes you wonder why you went down this path at all.

This life audit allows you to be honest about where you are, it tells you where you are and helps you make the decision on where you should be going.

Now it is not some sort of super natural phenomena or some sort of Ask Zoltar moment, it is a task that does what all best tasks do.

It takes your knowledge and experience and asks you to delve into the parts of your brain that sometimes we choose to ignore.

You know those parts – the "If I forget about it, it will go away" parts. It's the stuff we push away and don't want to deal with.

But it is also the stuff that we know we have to eventually deal with if we ever want to make decisions and move forwards with anything.

So here we go.

So just to remind you once more, please remember, pick up a pen, write in the book, make it relevant to you and your business.

This book hopefully is not only full of stories and my experiences, but also the activities that you can do to make a difference.

Take a look at the graphic: you can see there are eight categories.

Life Audit

Mark out of 10 - where 10 is perfect. Where are you now?

		Score
Business		
Bank Balance		
Network		
Career		
Friendship		
Relationship		
Fitness		
Rest & Relaxation		
	Total score out of 80	

Take time to go through this and score yourself from one to 10.

No one is going to see this. If you have borrowed the book or you think that someone else may be too cheap to buy their own copy, then undertake this task on a piece of paper.

I get that this is a pretty obvious task. Please don't give up on the book just yet because you think, "Ranking my life out of 10 – I thought this was a business book, not some weird self-help manual."

This exercise has more power than you will ever know and most importantly it's a great and safe place for you to start to be honest with yourself and where you are.

Remember when you are rating yourself, 10 is the best that things can be, and one is the worst.

Be honest with yourself. This exercise is just between me and you. You don't need to put a gloss on anything. The results are not going anywhere and no one is asking you to link to your Instagram story. Although if you want to post a picture of the book and tag me into it, I won't be complaining.

To help you with the process, I have broken down the areas to walk you through each one before you go ahead and rate everything 10 or one, depending.

The Business:

Where are you within your business? If you were really honest, where would you put yourself? Is it everything you wanted it to be, or not? There's no shame in admitting things aren't right, but you need to do something about it.

I don't want you to be too hard on yourself, but I do want you to be honest.

You could even break this down into five sub-categories and rank each of them out of two.

Add those numbers together and this will give you your figure out of ten.

Is your head hurting yet with all of these numbers, especially when we are only one chapter in already!

So you might think about these sub-categories:

Is the business meeting the aims or desires of your initial plan?
Does working in the business leave you feeling fulfilled?
Are you always reaching your business targets?
Do you clear your to do list each day?
Can you take a day off and still feel secure that nothing will happen to your business?

Remember, this task only works if you are honest with yourself in this particular moment.

The emphasis is on this particular moment.

Ask again tomorrow or in three weeks, three months or three years and things may look very different.

But In Cahoots is all about dealing with the here and now, don't be scared. We can change anything, we just have to know the things we want to change first.

Bank Balance:

This one is contentious one. I am always told by numerous people that money isn't everything.

You know what? I agree with that. But...

Money is something. Having enough or just enough so that you don't have to worry on a daily basis is everything you need to help you grow your business.

If you don't have quite enough to give you the security you need the problem is, you have no choice but to chase the money in your business just to get you through the day. Sometimes, this means that you are forced to make decisions you wouldn't if you had a little bit of security in the bank.

That security is not the same for everyone, however. For some it's £1, for others it's £100,000.

It really doesn't matter. Remember, for this task, it is whatever is the truth for you in this moment.

In 2018, I had a business partner whose mantra was always 'what is my exposure?' He had a limit of how much he was going to risk or invest into the business.

For all sorts of reasons, his level and my level of risk were completely different.

For example, at this particular time, cashflow looked awful, we were due a large tax payment and we still had the monthly expenses outgoing. Not only that, we had borrowed a large amount of money.

When we had our meeting, this partner asked his usual question 'What is my exposure?" and I gave him the figure of £100,000.

He nearly died. How had he let himself get to this point, where his top-most figure had always been £50,000?

For me the figure was £500,000. Not because of any great difference other than I had absolute faith in the business and could see the business as whole rather than in individualised parts. Also, I was younger and had at least twenty years to recover the money should things go wrong.

If you had ranked this partner's number, I have no doubt he would have been one at this point.

I would have ranked it somewhere near a seven

Partners in a business with the same level of risk and yet, so different in terms of the number ranking.

It meant we had to make some decisions on what we did with the business, though.

He was not comfortable with that level of exposure so he left the business and effectively gave us it back.

My exposure rose from £100,000 to £200,000 but it was still well within my top level of personal exposure at £500,000.

My ranking number did not change, it was still at 7 out of 10.

So let's now talk about you.

In the words of my old business partner, 'What's your exposure?' and more importantly, "What exposure are you happy with?"

What does your bank balance look like?

Is it really positive, or satisfactory but could be better?

What does 'better' look like?

Be ambitious and think of a number that stretches you and also acts as a goal for you to reach.

And give me your number – one being the worst and 10 the best. What do you look like?

Network:

Who I surround myself with is the key to any success I have had in business at all.

When people hear the word 'network', they often confuse it with the term 'networking', but that's not what we're talking about.

Your network is those key people who you couldn't do business without.

Not just business contacts.

To give you an example, I have two daughters and when both were small, we needed a childminder, Cath.

Cath was the most vital part of my network, because with her help I could concentrate on running my business, knowing that the two most precious things in my life were taken care of and taken care of well.

If I hadn't had Cath as part of my network, how would I have run my company?

So when you are thinking about your network, make a point of not just thinking about your traditional business network but all of the different elements that allow you to run your business on a day to day basis.

What does your current network look like? Is it a really positive business network or do you need to do something about it?

Are you surrounded by people who motivate you and are the best they can be as well?

Can you rely on your network when you need it?

Have you got someone in your network that will tell you the truth and give you an honest answer about where you and your business are?

Now remember to give yourself a score and write it down. As with all of the other sections, one is worst and ten is the best.

Career:

Now this one might seem like a funny one for a business owners book.

Career – isn't this for someone with a job?

I left my career behind to start a business!

Did you?

I always find it strange when people distinguish between running a business and having a career. For me they are both the same.

When you set out on your path of work, regardless of whether you are employed or self-employed, having a successful career is something we all aspire to.

A career, or a job, which makes a difference to someone or something.

This is no different when running your business.

If your career is that of business leader or even CEO or MD of a business, is this the career path for you?

Do you feel fulfilled?

Would you rather not have a career?

Where are you in your career?

Are you comfortable and confident?

Remember when you are ranking where you are with your career, one is worst and ten is best.

Now add this to the chart.

Friendships:

Friendships are an interesting one. Perhaps you are thinking this is much more personal than professional. You would be wrong, however I am thinking here about business friendships.

Those people you know will give you an honest answer and will feel comfortable doing so because you are friends, and they know you won't take any criticism personally.

These might not be the friends you grew up with or went to school with, but the friends you have made along your journey.

To illustrate this, if you remember right at the beginning of the book, I described my relationship with a lady named Helen, who was really my very first friend in business.

Move forwards thirty odd years, she is still a friend, and most importantly, a truthful sounding board whose opinion I really value.

I have others.

Here's an interesting thing though. Helen has never met my wife or children, even though I talk about them, and likewise I have never met her partner.

Even after all of these years we have a really strong and truthful business friendship and it's one friendship I value and cherish.

So when you are marking this part out of ten think about how by having strong friendships, it can often mean the difference between a strong business and a weak one.

You surround yourself with like-minded people who support and promote you.

Now what number would you rank yourself at?

Relationships:

We talked and ranked ourselves out of ten last time with regards to friendships in business.

This time we are talking about your personal relationships.

Partners, friends and family – your support network outside of your business.

Where are you in your relationships?

Do you have strong, supportive relationships around you or is this something that needs to be worked on?

Honestly, I am very close to my mum and she is supportive in her own way and yet despite the fact I have been self-employed my whole life, she will still now and again ask me when I will get a proper job like my two teacher sisters.

This is not meant detrimentally and comes from a caring place and yet I know as much as I love my Mum, the support I need is just not available in the way I need it.

You know, those people you share stuff with and take advice from? They're not necessarily business friends, but the 'framily' you choose to spend time with. They listen to your musings and you listen to theirs.

FRAMILY - The definition of Framily is those friends that become like family. You know those people you share stuff with and take advice from, that are not necessarily business friends, but the framily you chose to spend time with, they listen to your musings and you listen to theirs.

So again out of ten how would you rate the current state of those relationships?

Fitness:

As anyone who knows me will attest, fitness is not my natural state of mind.

I can smell chocolate, crisps, dips and all manner of unhealthy products at fifty paces and yet I know the power of movement on the ability to grow a business.

By fitness, I don't mean going to the gym every day, although it could mean that. I mean doing some sort of exercise, gentle exercise included.

For me the biggest pleasure that helped me grow my business most was the simple act of walking my dog each day.

Not only was he the best listener in the world, but just the act of having to walk him twice a day, gave me the opportunity to plan for the day ahead or reflect on the day that had just happened.

It also gave me the time to be away from my business to really to really think about how I was going to work on it.

So fitness, whether that's walking, running, yoga or going to the gym, is very important.

Physical fitness aside, some sort of mental training is also very important. For me that is meditation and something called creative visualisation.

The time to de-stress in a quiet moment is everything I need to be re-invigorated and rebalanced and ready to go.

So when we talk about fitness, we are talking about both physical and mental fitness.

Rate yourself out of ten now, where 10 is the most physically and mentally fit you can be and one is worst.

Now where did I hide the Dairy Milk!!!!

Rest and Relaxation:

The best lesson I was ever given and one which I find the hardest to follow personally is the ability to rest and switch off from my businesses.

I have to physically plan time and make sure that no work disturbances can happen.

It's why I love cruise holidays. Those days at sea mean no one can get through on your on your mobile or email unless you actively choose to let them.

But taking the time to rest and relax is the key to your businesses growth success.

A rested and relaxed mind is a mind ready to identify new ideas and new ways to improve and add to current business goals.

A rested body allows the space for new developments to happen and most of all a rested body allows for the flow of creativity.

Are you at rest?

Do you take the time to relax and make space in your diary for re-invigoration?

Do you take the time to rest and relax?

This is really important to help you build your business and give you personal security in terms of where you are. You need to be able to switch off.

Now rate yourself out of ten. Remember ten is the best you can be at this.

Now what

Once you have a score out of ten for each of the eight areas, add all of the scores up to give you the total number out of eighty.

The trick now is to reflect on where you got the lowest numbers.

That's where we are going to start.

Your lowest number.

The aim of this book is not to get you to eighty. I think perhaps that number for so many of us is unobtainable, but as close to eighty as we possibly can.

So let's start with the lowest number first. Write down on a piece of paper which section that number appears on.

Now, I'd recommend starting with this to help us set some goals.

First things first. What do you have to do to raise that number to ten?

Write down three goals that would get you to ten if you achieved them.

We have the first three growth targets we are going to need for In Cahoots.

Well done.

See? I told you this programme was not rocket science but small, implementable steps that will mean You and your business grow and flourish.

What shall we do next?

P.S. Remember you should reassess your figures often, but at the very least every three to six months.

Chapter Three
Time

OK, this is the very scary chapter, where we talk about time.

In all of my years in business, and for 99% of business owners I've ever spoken to, time and time management have been the biggest areas that people have needed help with.

Here's the thing with time; no matter how old you are, wherever you live in the world, or your gender, we all have three things in common. We were all born, we will all die and we all have twenty-four hours in a day and fifty two weeks in a year.

And yet some people are able to take those twenty four hours and achieve great things, where others just don't have the time to fit in some of the most basic tasks.

I fit into the latter category. I never seem to have enough time, so these two tasks really help me understand my time and my time management skills.

This part of the book looks at how much time you have left to achieve everything you want to.

In the graphic the 82 clocks represent the average lifespan of a UK resident (one for each year of your life). How scary is that? Just by knowing that fact makes you think about time in a different way. You might feel differently if you are 22, but at 52 – 82 does not feel that far away.

How Much Time do You Have?

In the UK, the national retirement age is 67 so we'll use that as our guide to help us work out how much time we have left for work.

Most of us would like to retire at some point, but even if you don't, even if you want to work until you drop, this first activity is made just for you.

So let's work on the assumption you would like to retire at 67. This means you need from the clock sheet to remove 15 clocks.

Just to be clear: we are removing the number of clocks you've already had or don't need.

By removing 15 clocks, that means we have sixty seven left on the graphic.

Remember if you want to retire earlier, you need to remove the corresponding number of clocks.

So for example if you wanted to retire at 50, you would need to remove 32 clocks and so on.

Next the hard part.

Depending on your age, you may not want to share this part. Remember though for the purpose of this book and yourself, we will keep this just between us.

You are HOW old?

Sorry just kidding.

The next step is to remove the number of clocks that represent your age.

So if you are 21 remove twenty one clocks, if you are 45 clocks remove forty five and so on.

Are you feeling nervous yet?

Now remember in the previous task I asked you to write down three goals. If I asked you to write down your overriding business goal, what would that be?

Now have a look at the clocks.

The unremoved clocks tell you exactly how long you have to achieve these goals.

If you're 45, you'll have 22 clocks left, or 22 years to achieve your goals if you choose to retire at 67.

Remember, the earlier you want to retire, the more you have to achieve in less time. The further away you are from retirement, the more time you have.

Depending on what you want to achieve, that could be plenty of time, or not enough time, to do everything.

If you decide to retire earlier, then you have fewer clocks left. It's important to be realistic with your time.

And be honest.

Look at the time you have left. Is it realistic to have set the business goals you have or do you need more or less time to achieve these outputs?

Now you know how long you have, do you need to revise those plans at all or can you reach those targets?

Please don't change the time left, unless you really want to. It's easier to revise targets than it is to lose years.

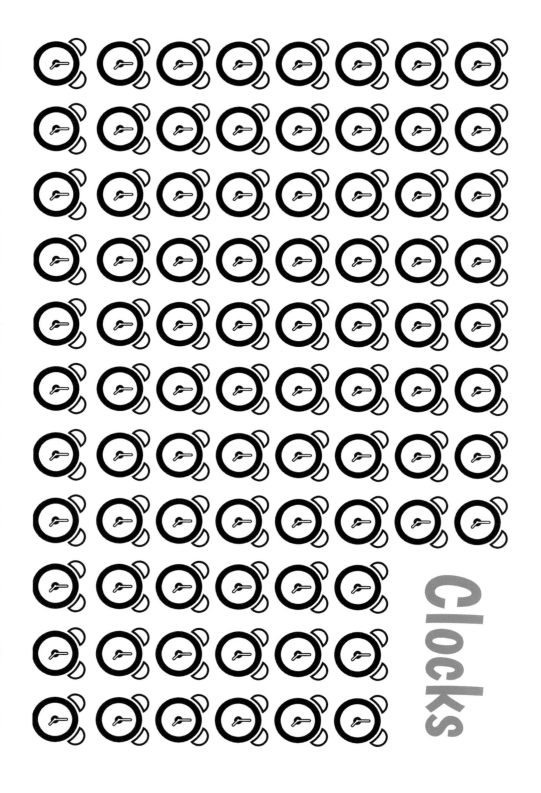

Clocks

Why Should You do This?

Doing this exercise helps you to think about your ideas – your goals and your mission. When you do it, you become much more focused on what you need to do to retire, to build your business or grow it. You can see the finite amount of time that you have left to work.

The clocks are important because they're ticking down, and it's a universal truth that all of us have these clocks, representing each year of our lives. We may live to be 97 and have more clocks, but on average we'll live until 82.

Work out your own average and plot in your ambitions, targets and goals to see how much time you need to allocate to each. If you have a turnover target, what are the steps to get you there and what timescale do you have?

Time Management

Everybody has 24 hours in the day. It's a universal truth. The most successful people have 24 hours, as do the least successful. It's what you do with those 24 hours that counts.

How to Maximise Your Time

We're going to look at how to use the time you have available every day to get the most work don. More importantly, we'll look at looking at how to make sure you do the work you should be doing, rather than the stuff that you want to do, or the stuff that takes up your time.

Scheduling

Urgent Not Important	Urgent and Important
Not Urgent Not Important	**Not Urgent Important**

Take your to do list every morning to highlight in the colours above.
Eliminate all yellow features. Start with pink then move onto green.
Repeat this each day.

Four Areas for Time Management

1. Urgent, not important
2. Urgent and important
3. Not urgent and not important
4. Not urgent, but important

What to do

Every morning when you sit down and do your to-do list (and from a time management point of view, you should do this every day!) take out four, different coloured highlighters, one for each box on the graphic. You can use the same colours as in the example, or pick your own.

Every morning, take your to-do list and the pen which corresponds to the appropriate box colour, and highlight anything which is urgent and has to be done, but is not important. These are tasks which are not business critical.

Next, highlight everything which is urgent and important, the things which will make your business grow or that you have to do.

Repeat the process for those things which are not urgent and not important and the things that are urgent but not business critical.

These might be things with a long lead-in time and you can do in the next few days.

Next Steps

Take your to-do list and look for everything that's marked as not urgent and not important.

The first thing you're going to do is to eliminate them out of your day – you won't be doing them.

Cross them out, lose them, you won't miss them.

If they're not urgent or important, why are they on your to-do list?

You have to be really critical of what's going onto it. Be strong with yourself and be disciplined. It is really easy to add lots of things onto a to do list, it is not so easy to be able to cross them off.

Then, look at everything which is urgent and important to your business growth and daily work.

Now move them up in your to-do list as they're the first jobs you need to do every day.

Next, let's find and define the not urgent but important tasks, and move them down to third on the list.

Finally, we are going to identify the urgent and not important. These tasks should be second.

Do this exercise every day, highlighting your to-do list with your chosen set of colours.

Remember, the not urgent and not important tasks need to be eliminated from the list.

The aim of both of these tasks, both the clocks and the time management elements, is to give you back some of the precious time you need to be able to function and achieve your goals.

Remember In Cahoots is all about setting achievable targets that can be reached. To set targets that you will never reach will only ever end up demotivating you and mean that you will forget the discipline of both the time management techniques and the overall goal setting.

Personally, I set my to do list at no more than ten items.

I know if I set any more than that, I will never reach the conclusion of the list and I will spend the next day feeling demotivated as I was unable to remove things from the list.

That number can be whatever you feel comfortable with, but most importantly please be realistic with yourself and give yourself some time to respond to changing events and priorities.

Chapter Four
Ideas Generation

Ideas generation is the life blood of your business. It's how you develop, grow and change.

Please remember it's not necessarily about new ideas; it can be looking at and expanding on existing ideas.

I would go as far as to say, 90% of your time should be spent generating ideas and solutions around your current work and 10% on new ideas or new routes to market.

The graphic below is base upon one I was shown at Babson College. It's been a game-changer both for me and for several businesses I've worked with, and I think it's a great way of illustrating how to come up with new ideas.

You can use it to look at what you've already got available in your business and what you can develop.

It's a great way of placing ideas and generating new ones, but most importantly, it's an activity that takes only 5 minutes to run and can give you new avenues and directions for existing products and services you had never even thought of.

Types of Ideas

For this process and activity we are going to categorise our areas of ideas into three.

1. Grounded
2. Blue Sky
3. Spaced Out

Grounded Ideas

A 'grounded idea' is something that you can do now, which already exists within your business and you can grow. It's something that you operate on every day, you know about and can deal with.

To give you an example, in my own business, the thing I do the most of is train business owners.

So, my grounded idea might be, 'training people on how to grow their businesses.

I can deliver this future and am doing so now with existing customers.

Spaced Out Ideas

A 'spaced-out idea' is the fun one. If you had all the budget in the world, no limitations, a team of people to help you and anything you wanted, this is what you'd create. It's your ideal – something you'd love to do and feel passionate about

So for example a spaced-out idea for me is to take twelve business owners on a worldwide business retreat around the world, for twelve weeks, examining different ideas and different ways companies in other countries do business.

This would be free to the participants and I would be able to identify the businesses I would like to take with me.

Blue Sky Ideas

In between these two is a 'blue sky' idea. It's halfway between because it's achievable and it's something you want to do, and it's also a new idea or development for your business.

For me recently a Blue Sky idea was to deliver our Inspiration USA programme, which is a combination of a grounded idea, delivering business growth training to business owners and a Spaced out idea, but taking these business owners for a week to the USA to learn from other business owners and other business support processes.

Truly, this was an idea I came up with.

Another Real-Life Idea Example

Here's a true-life example to help you understand this better, and we'll look at somebody everybody knows - Richard Branson.

His grounded idea could be Virgin Atlantic, an airline which fly routes around the world. The Atlantic part predominantly between the UK and the USA.

As he wanted to come up with something outstanding, world-class and the world's first, he could have examined this process and look to a spaced-out idea, being a flight to Mars.

His critics may have said it was a fantasy and he'd never be able to do it, but in this process this doesn't matter at all.

Remember spaced-out ideas have no limitations at all and no way of stopping them. Money, talent, technology and any other barrier are not allowed with a spaced-out idea.

When we do this task it's really easy to fall back into the place of trying to be realistic.

We don't need realism here, we need fantasy, no limits and an openness to really dream.

I always like to think of developing the spaced out idea as that song by the Monkees and latterly by the giant Shrek – Daydream Believer. For this task that's what I would like you to be

P.S. I know you are still singing the song. Now try and get it out of your head today!!!!

Ok back to Richard Branson.

He may have reflected and said, "You're right with technology the way it is today, I'm not able to do it. If I had unlimited resources, then of course I'd be able to do it, but I don't."

So he decided to marry the Grounded idea and the spaced-out idea together and he took his idea down a level, and came up with his blue-sky option – a manned space flight – which became his company Virgin Galactic.

He took a true, new idea within his business that wasn't massively removed from his original idea, but wasn't so far removed that it was spaced-out and something he would never reach.

Isn't this amazing? Taking an idea that is unreachable and adapting it and making fit your current business.

Remember when you do this, it's not just new ideas, almost more importantly it's taking your existing ideas and adding to them and developing things further.

What Ideas do you have?

What are the current, grounded ideas in your business?
Who are your markets and what are your routes to them?
What are the products and services you offer every day?

Be honest when you look at your offerings, because some things will be working and others won't.

Come up with as many spaced-out ideas as you can.

These are the things you've always dreamed about and think of as flights of fancy.

You've got no budget restrictions and no limitations, so what do you want to achieve?

It's your heart's desire.

Now, and perhaps most importantly, what comes in the middle of your grounded idea and your spaced-out idea?

This is your blue-sky idea, and something you can add to your new to do list to take forward next. Remember this is a quick activity and you will only need to spend five minutes on it, but you could come up with something great.

Make sure you do this exercise quickly and without thinking about it too much.

It's a fun activity and one which I think you should be repeating at least once a month when you are looking at growth.

It's okay to have your feet on the ground, but your eyes should be looking at the big blue sky. Try some space exploration and reenter with a more attractive, bigger blue sky.

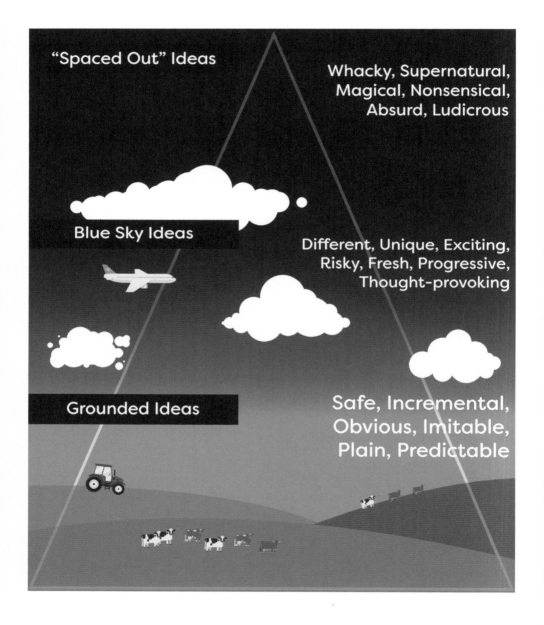

Growth Strategy

We have been looking at ideas, but we also need a strategy for our growth and a way of putting all of these things we are establishing on our to-do lists into a viable strategy.

This task gives you the first starting-off point to think about where your growth is going to come from.

Here, you can develop a plan which is based around what's going on in your market at any given time.

Develop A Strategy For Growth

TRENDS

What is happening in your industry at the moment?

STRENGTHS

What are yours and your businesses core strengths?

WEAKNESSES

What are yours and your businesses core weaknesses?

Trends

Trends and knowing the trends happening in your marketplace can be invaluable when trying to develop growth and sustainability. Identifying those trends on a regular basis can be the key to this success.

What trends are happening within your market, and also outside it?

Look nationally and internationally for inspiration. Remember, there is not only you doing the thing that you are doing and if there is, you might be creating the trend that other people will jump onto.

To give you an example, in 2020 in terms of areas and trends in food, the rise in vegan food offerings has seen a 340% increase in the vegan food market. This presents a huge opportunity for many food production companies and interestingly has lead to a trend in increased veganism.

Contextualise it by thinking about where you are in your business and where it is in the world.

It's like going back to the start and thinking about market research, because this is something that's continuous, especially from a growth perspective.

For example, if you started your business 15 years ago and that's the last time you did any market research, then you need start making time for it now, and on a regular basis.

It's impossible that nothing has changed in those 15 years.

What was happening only six months ago is different to what's happening now. Here is the other thing as well, sometimes when we have been in business for a long time the lazier we get and we suppose we know the answers.

Now is the time to forget your preconceptions and start again.

Identify with any trends that may have changed over recent months. Likewise, your growth strategy is a living, breathing document.

What it is not is a business plan, so don't file it in a drawer and forget about it.

It can be as short as a single page, but it will give you a clear plan and defined areas to develop so you can grow your business.

Think about what's happening and where, and how you'll find out about and access it.

Identify any opportunity you could make or take advantage of from any changing circumstances.

Your Business and Personal Strengths

Take time to review your strengths, or core competencies if you like, and also that of your team, if you have one.

What are the things within your business which you could develop, build upon and use?

Strengths are things which are easy to sell, are a transferable skill into another market or can be used to develop a new route to market.

Build on your existing strengths and see what else you could do with them.

When you've looked at trends, is there a diversification of your market where you could apply your strengths or core competencies?

Be honest with yourself but not too hard. I know I keep repeating this, but honestly being honest with yourself in these circumstances is the key to building a successful growing business.

Self-evaluation and self-determination will do nothing but good, both for you and your growing business. Assess yourself and your key skills regularly.

Weakness

Don't pull your business apart or be negative about it, but do be honest with yourself.

Looking at the weaknesses in your business can be the thing that increases the growth trajectory.

Recognising what a weakness is and improving on it is really important.

Conversely, recognising a weakness and realising you'll never be able to do something about it, but looking at other core strengths you could build on to help minimise that weakness, may be the way that you build your business.

Being honest about your strengths and weaknesses is the way that you'll grow your business.

When you sit down and think about developing a growth strategy, these are the three key areas to focus on.

Only by identifying these three areas can you begin to develop a cohesive growth plan, but it's definitely worth doing, and it's very exciting when you do.

Make sure you write these things down and regularly (at least every three months) go back and review them.

When it comes to developing or re-developing those ideas, this will be the key skill to establishing the success of this process.

Be critical but not judgemental and most importantly always reward yourself with a treat after you have undertaken these processes.

I always find a bar of chocolate does the trick for me.

You can see I am easily bribed.

Chapter Five
Brand Values

In this instance we are looking at brand values from a digital point of view.

When you create digital content, think about the brand values that you're trying to communicate to your customer from a marketing point of view.

Why are Brand Values Important?

Brand values are the very core of your business, the thing you want people to remember you for.

Think of a famous brand. They always have some key words that they would use to describe their product or service.

OK for the purpose of this exercise I am going to go old fashioned and mention the slogan that the Mars Bar used for a number of years. (Remember I bring everything back to chocolate).

For years the brand used the slogan, 'A Mars a day helps you work, rest and play.'

The brand value they were trying to establish was that a Mars Bar could be bought and eaten for any eventuality.

It's another of those slogans that will now stick in your head and if you are of a certain age you are probably singing it now, sorry.

How would you describe your product or service?

For any content you put out there about your business, there are six areas that you need to consider when you're creating it.

1. If seven of your customers were in a room together, how would you like them to describe you?

Be as honest as you can when you answer this.

What are the words that you would like them to be using about you?

Pretend that you're not there, and think about what they're saying. If you think they'd be saying something negative, why is that?

2. What is it that makes you different?

What is it that makes you stand out from everyone else?

The one thing you're not allowed to use to help you stand out is cost, so take that away as a brand value.

How do you differ from your nearest competitor?

3. What do you like to do the most?

Thinking about your business, what motivated you to start it?

What is it that makes you different and that you love to do?

Identify those key areas, because from a content creation point of view, your passion and enthusiasm will come across.

4. If a customer uses your product or service, in what way are they rewarded?

It might not be cost, or the product or service.

What words would they use about the feelings that they get?

When you think about your brand values, feelings are really important, because customers choose a product or service not on its viability but because of the way it makes them feel.

5. What qualities within your business, product or service are you most proud of?

What makes you puff out your chest and feel great about what you're delivering?

What are those qualities?

Make a list of them to help you with your content creation.

6. What one word would you use to describe your product or service?

You can only choose one word, and it will be the key to you building content around your brand value. What is it that makes you feel really excited and passionate, and that you would like to tell the world about from your product, service, or business perspective?

When we're talking about content creation and brand values from a digital perspective, we're answering six questions, and it's important to keep each of them in mind every time you create something new.

Remember this establishment of a brand value is going to be reflected in everything you put out online across multiple platforms, so you must think it is a true reflection of the messages and your ethos you are trying to portray.

Brand Values

List 10 words that describe your brand values.

1

2

3

4

5

6

7

8

9

10

Pick the 3 most important words from the list.

1

2

3

Create a Facebook post for your product/service that includes the 3 words.

_____

_____

_____

_____

_____

Chapter Six
Identifying Your Customer & Creating an Empathy Map

Identifying a customer is really important, because if you just think you know who your customer is, you can often be wrong.

I'm going to share a couple of real-life examples with you.

In Cahoots (my business) is a great example. When we set it up, I thought I'd have a 50/50 male/female split. In fact, 76% of the audience for my video training and other content are female entrepreneurs, with only 24% male.

What is the problem with that?" you may ask. Intrinsically, the answer is nothing. However, it does mean that I need to tailor my content in a particular way, of change the sort of content I'm putting out if I want to attract more males to the group.

As it was, it didn't actually matter. I carried on, and the split is now 29% male and 71% female.

However, I know now that having a predominantly female.

I base my sub categories on interests rather than gender and this really helps me target the interests of the members of the group.

Why it's Important to Know Your Customer

So why is that important?

The message we give and the way we communicate might be different. That may not necessarily be the case in this instance, but for you and your business, it could be.

There is no business in the world that has 100% of everyone as customers.

Often people will say: "My customers are everyone, because everybody wants my product or service."

That's simply not true! By identifying who your customer is, you'll actually sell more, because the message and brand you give, and the way you communicate with those customers, is more important than anything else.

How do You Identify Customers?

There are a number of ways to identify customers: are they male, female or a mix?

If there is a mix, what percentage of it is male and female?

How much income do they have?

Is there a particular income bracket you're aiming for?

Here's another example, this time with clothing.

I live in Middlesbrough in the North East of England, I would say the best place in the world to live. (I know there is only me saying it).

There are a number of department stores, and you wouldn't expect to pay the same price for the same product in each store.

For example, if you went into Primark to buy a plain, white, scoop-necked T-shirt, how much would you expect to pay?

Let's be honest, if you were paying more than £3, you'd think: "Wow, this is really expensive in Primark!"

But if you looked for the same item in Next, you wouldn't expect to pay the same as you would in Primark.

You may pay between £5 and £8.

Likewise, if you then went and bought a designer T-shirt, from someone like Armani, you wouldn't expect to pay what you paid in Next or Primark.

The Customer Base

Is the customer base for those T-shirts exactly the same?

Definitely not.

They are all customers buying white T-shirts, but the persona is very different. Even if that T-shirt is made in exactly the same factory, the same way and with the same grade of cotton, the customer who buys the Armani T-shirt will not be the customer who goes into Primark.

By identifying who those customers are and what their motivation is, you will be able to develop your customer base.

You need to be clear on these things when it comes to creating content and marketing to them.

Along with gender and economic factors, age is also key. When you know all these things about your customer, the details will help you decide where you brand your product or service and how you speak to them.

The fun part of this exercise is creating the persona, so you can describe who your persona (or avatar) is.

In our training sessions, we use a skeleton called Alex, and he's useful because he can be any customer.

Think about your customer.

What do they look like, where do they shop and what do they buy?

Where and how do they live?

Knowing the customer in that amount of detail will help you market, develop and grow your business.
An empathy map is a tool we can use when we're looking to undertake market research to grow and build a product, service or business.

The empathy map is like a road map, easy to understand and refer to when you're speaking to existing or current customers.

The Four Elements of the Empathy Map

There are four main elements to an empathy map. In the middle is the customer, and each element needs to be taken into consideration whenever you talk to them.

1. What do They Say?

What is it that they say? When you ask them questions, what is it that you think you can gain from their answers that will help you change the aspects of the things you want to grow?

You're asking them specific questions, and you want them to talk and display their feelings.

You'll be reading their body language when they answer you – are they comfortable and at ease?

Are they telling you things, or do you think you need to dig a little deeper into what the problem is and where they need help?

2. What Action do They Take?

When they say they're going to do something, whether it's to buy from you, become repeat customers or just have a conversation with you, do they actually do it?

Are there any times where you've been in a position where somebody has said to you: "I love your product or service, but I'm just not ready at the moment to do what you want"?

What are the reasons that they give you for doing that?

From an empathy point of view, is there a general pattern to the answers people give you for not buying your product or service?

When you're thinking about growth, are they things you can overcome or do they need more work?

3. What do They Think About Before Buying?

What does your customer think about before they buy from you?

What is it in their thought process that changes them from potentially a sale to somebody who is a definite?

Do they go away and think about it or do they make a snap judgement?

Are there words you could use to help them make a decision?

4. How Does Your Business Make Them Feel?

Have you ever asked your customer how your business or offering makes them feel?

What words would they use to describe the feelings of buying your product or service?

Feelings are key when it comes to making a buying decision. If you can identify what that feeling is, whether it makes them feel good, less nervous or less worried, what are the words they use?

Use your empathy map to decide the four key areas that provide the buying signals.

Yes, it's market research, but it's also very much a great sales tool that you can use. Once you can truly out yourself in the shoes of your customer and really identify what it is they require and need, you will find yourself, adopting their tone of voice, the ideas and thought patterns they hold and most importantly using the words and phrasing for things they like.

The Empathy Map

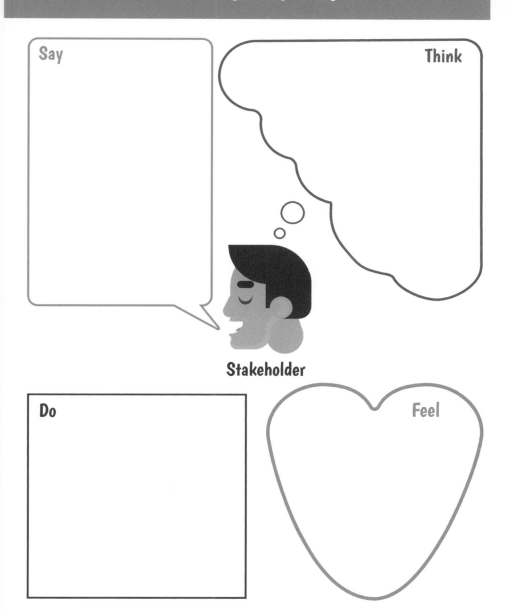

Say

Think

Stakeholder

Do

Feel

Chapter Seven
Value Proposition &
Differentiation

Why is the value proposition important to your business?

For me, I always think it's like the stake in the ground, the flag at the summit. It's the thing that you've identified as the primary way you'll grow your business, product or service.

You are identifying what exactly is valuable to you.

The Seven Core Areas of Your Value Proposition

You need to think carefully about each of the following seven areas when it comes to developing your value proposition.

1. Who is Your Audience?

Think about this from a specific point of view, not in general terms.

Who is your target audience?

Who's buying your product or service?

If you're not currently selling anything, who is it that contacts you about your future offering?

Look at who's recently contacted you or bought from you. Is there a common denominator between them?

2. What is the Need or Opportunity of the Customers?

What need are you trying to or already service?

Is there something specifically that's been asked of you?

When somebody contacts you or you tell someone you're meeting for the first time about what you do, what is the opportunity?

What is the key word? Identifying the key need or the opportunity is really important.

3. Identifying Your Product or Service

Identify what your product or service is in a concise manner.

I always think of it this way: If you have a five-year-old child in front of you and you have to use 10 words or fewer to describe what your product or service is or does, how would you do that?

Take the time to identify, within that restriction, exactly what your product is.

Do it now – in no more than ten words, what does your product or service do? - read it to someone who knows nothing about your business, have they understood what it is your business does?

Be honest and revise it if they didn't get it at the first reading.

4. Which Category Does Your Product or Service Fall into?

For example, I'd say: "My product or service falls into the category of 'business to business', because the majority of my customers are other businesses."

Perhaps your category is 'business to consumer', 'direct retail' or 'online retail.'

Be specific.

This doesn't have to apply to all of your customers, but which category do the majority fall into?

5. The One Compelling Reason Why People Buy from You

Identify the one reason why people will buy your product or service.

Identifying this key factor is really important, particularly when you think about marketing spend and the message that you're going to try to give.

Is it based on price? On quality? Or something completely different?

6. The Primary Competitive Alternative

What is the primary competitive alternative to your business?

If someone doesn't buy from you, where do they go and what do they buy?

What is the product or service offered by your main competition?

Be specific – is it something in the local area, is it national or is it international?

7. The Primary Differentiator

What is the primary differentiator between you and that competitor?

Once you've identified who your competitor is, what is that differentiates you from them?

Be honest, this doesn't have to be all negative things, in some instances they may have a positive competitive advantage over you. That's not the problem. The problem is that you haven't been able to identify and compensate for that fact.

Value Proposition

Create a short paragraph when thinking about either your business, your product or your service.

Think about the 7 areas we are covering:

1) For...   Who is the target audience!

2) Who... What is the need or opportunity you are servicing!

3) The... The product or the service is.

4) Is a... The product/service falls into the category of

5) That... What is the compelling reason people will buy the product or service?

6) Unlike... What is the primary competitive alternative?

7) Our product/service... What is the primary differentiation

_____

_____

_____

_____

_____

Differentiation

Differentiation is important in your business because it sets you apart from your competitors.

You need to work out what your points of differentiation are and what's different about your product, service or business from the people who do something similar or your competitors.

The Top 10 Benefits of Your Business

What are the top 10 benefits of your business?

Take a piece of paper and write them down.

As with everything we do with In Cahoots, the very act of writing things down is the thing that makes the difference.

So when you are thinking about the benefits your business can offer your customer or your potential customer, these are some of the areas you may want to think about.

Do people really like your service?

Are you always punctual?

Think about the benefits you provide to your customers?

If someone uses your products or services what will they gain from it?

Are there any physical benefits a customer would gain?

This should be an easy list for you to write!

What would a customer say about you and your business?

Take the time to write them down. Remember we need ten things, no more, no less!

The Top Three

Now we are going to take the top three things from your list.

What are the three benefits that you think are most important about your business?

Make a note now.

Then, take those three items and phone at least five of your customers.

You read that right.

I would like for you to get onto the telephone right now and call five of your customers.

I know you're reading this thinking, "I'll do it later. How will he know if I do it or not? Why should I bother?

You have committed to this book and you have committed to proving to me that if you follow this system you will see growth in your business, so do it now and don't delay.

Say to them: "I'm doing some research in my business. These are the things that I think are the best benefits that we offer. Do you agree?"

And make sure you listen to what they say!

Do they say, "Yep, we completely agree", or do they say, "Actually, the thing that we really think is a benefit of using your business is..."

Make sure you listen carefully and write down the things that people say about you. This is the best thing you can do in the whole of the book I THINK!

Don't pick a customer you know will give you the answer you want to hear, pick a customer that you don't know what the answer will be. A customer you don't know very well, a customer that doesn't necessarily want to please you.

Your Nearest Competitor

Who is your nearest competitor?

Don't say you don't have one, because everybody does.

It doesn't mean they do exactly the same as you, but they're an alternative choice for your customer.

This applies whether you offer products or services, work in retail or manufacturing.

Customers have choices.

You may know that they can't get what they want from the competitors, but they don't.

Who is your competitor, and what are the three most valuable benefits that they provide?

Do the research, look at your competitors online and offline presence.

Try and buy something from them.

Be honest with yourself. If you think that they are doing something better, write it down. If you think that you are doing something better, again, write it down.

Then, and this might sound odd, phone somebody who has bought from you before, and then ask them why they chose you and not your competitor?

Remember: don't be scared, people like to help.

And don't phone your Aunty Mavis or someone that you know, call somebody who will give you a truthful answer, not just one they hope you want to hear.

This is market research on the competition. Obviously, you're not going to give them that research, but you need to know what the points of differentiation are between your business and that of your competitors.

The only way you can do that is by asking.

Start with yourself, your benefits, what you want to achieve and what you want your customers to say about you, and then you do the research by asking people. Don't suppose you know exactly what it is your customers want.

By doing the differentiation exercise, you're effectively redoing your market research. As a trading business, you'll hopefully have done some research before you started, and now you're up and running you're doing some more.

You're thinking about your competitor and finding out what it is people didn't like about them and why they chose you instead. You don't need to know what they did like about them (if anything).

Create a Statement

Using the information you've gleaned from the two exercises above, come up with a statement that best describes your business and the differentiation of your business between yourself and your competitor.

That statement is your selling tool. It's what you need to let your potential customers know going forward – why they should use you. You've done the research and you have something to sell. You've created the words through your own research.

Differentiation is really important within your business, and it's also important to carry on doing it in six-month cycles, so make time in your diary to do these exercises again so you know if anything has changed.

Make the most of the knowledge you can gain for free and use and exploit the data that you are collecting to grow and build your business.

DIFFERENTIATION

A

Using your benefits list, record below the three most valuable benefits you provide to your customer.

1. _____

2. _____

3. _____

B

List your nearest competitor _____ and then record below the most valuable benefits they provide.

1. _____

2. _____

3. _____

C

Using the information from above, now write a statement tht details your "favorable points of differentiation": Essentially, you are stating why your offering is better than who you view as your nearest competitor.

_____

_____

_____

_____

Chapter Eight
SWOT & PEST

Nobody enjoys doing a SWOT analysis and if you've got one in your business plan, you probably thought you'd never have to do one again.

It's not interesting to do a SWOT, you won't have used it since you did it, and it's not something you do on a regular basis.

I just told you a lie. SWOT is interesting and is important in your business.

It is a brilliant tool in identifying areas of growth, both personal and professional and most of all it is something that can be done fairly quickly, although the research we have done in previous chapters should help with the delivery of this.

Remember, get out that pen and get ready to write into the book again, because this book only works if you join in.

I'm a preacher for SWOT and PEST – they're the things that make me smile!

They make me smile because with these two tasks you can almost spot where your areas of growth should be, both personally and professionally.

GET OUT THAT PEN!

SWOT Analysis

Strengths	Weaknesses

Opportunities	Threats

Strengths

What are your strengths within the business?

If you have a team, don't include them in this process, it's just about you.

Is a strength that your leadership skills are amazing, or your sales skills?

The biggest strength for a lot of entrepreneurs and business owners is ideas.

It doesn't have to be a learned skill, it can be your everyday strength.

By identifying these, you'll be clear on what the strengths are throughout the business.

Personal or professional, these key strengths are the things that will help you grown and develop your business as well as help you personally get to the place you are aiming towards.

Weaknesses

This is a difficult one, because you don't always want to admit to your weaknesses.

Or, you might be a really negative person who talks about weaknesses all the time.

Just be real about this.

A lot of the time, when people own businesses, they find it easy to talk about their weaknesses and not so easy to talk about their strengths.

If that's the case, you need to temper that.

If your weakness is the same as your strength, you need to remove it.

Think about realistic weaknesses, such as time management.

What are the things you haven't got going on?

What would be the things your customers would point out that would be your weaknesses?

For example, I am the worlds biggest procrastinator. Things get done and done well, but always at the last minute and always with a modicum of stress, when actually with better planning and preparation things could be much less stressful.

Opportunities

What opportunities can you bring to your business in terms of growth?

It could be new ideas, or commitment.

These are things that you personally bring to the business.

It doesn't mean that you do all of them, it just means you identify them.

Where are the opportunities you can spot? Remember, in an earlier activity we looked at developing ideas and spotting the opportunities around 'grounded', blue sky and spaced-out. It was you that was able to spot those opportunities. It's a gift.

Threats

What are the biggest threats that you bring to your business?

This is an interesting one. For instance, is it that you can't let go and give the work to someone else, or because you don't trust others?

Is it that there's only you, and if you do fall down that hole there's nobody to take over?

Is the threat that you don't have a business process model, so if you bring somebody in, people don't know exactly what it is that they're doing?

Are the threats external or internal?

What do they look like?

When you have written in all four of the boxes, I want you to think about this. With this particular SWOT we have concentrated on the internal threats and yet we all know that many of the threats we face are externally driven. How do we deal with those?

PEST

Most people complete a PEST or something similar when they start their business, and don't see why it matters to business growth.

To me, though, it's the most exciting part, because it's the thing that influences all of your decisions.

If you know PEST, you can have a workable growth model.

In the graphic, you can see the four quadrants that make up the analysis.

We are going to complete each section in relation to your business.

GET OUT THAT PEN AGAIN

Why PEST is Important

Your business doesn't operate in a silo.

There are lots of things in the world which will have an influence on your business which are important to be aware of.

When you make business growth decisions, you can't make them on your own. Look at what else is happening.

PEST - The Key To Business Growth Success

Political	Economic

Social	Technology

Political

You may feel you have no interest in politics, but it will have an impact on your business.

A recent, major political storm in the UK is Brexit, which we know will have an impact on business for at least the next 10 years.

What impact will that have?

How will you transport your goods and services?

Will you need VISAs or perhaps identity cards?

How will you employ staff from the EU, or will you lose staff from the EU?

Knowing what's happening politically will have a great impact, because it can show you opportunities as well as highlighting issues.

Political changes aren't always problems and can sometimes be positive.

Economic

What's happening with the economy can have an impact on your business, whether it's locally, nationally or internationally.

As an example, the financial crash in 2008 resulted in many banks going out of business.

The ripples weren't just in the financial market, but right through the economy.

Furthermore, the impact wasn't just on the UK economy but those of many other countries in the world.

Buying decisions were made on the basis of those economics, and were things which couldn't be dealt with on a macro level – they needed national input.

Economically as a result of the Covid pandemic, again, we are going to have to take into account the things that may now need to added into place for the next ten years or so economically, knowing what the financial impact may be can have a positive or negative impact on your business or industry.

Social

Socially, things change all the time, and there are opportunities when you know what's going on.

Again, this can be local, national or international.

You can find ways to train people or bring them into your business, for instance.

What are the changes that could have a positive or negative effect on your growth plans?

Socially, as a result of the pandemic, there has been a huge shift to online delivery. What social impact will this have on your business?

Will you need to change the way you meet people?

What happens when things go back to normal? Does everything go back to the way it was?

Do you want it to go back to the way it was?

Technology

The easiest example of this is the mobile phone.

In the year 2000 it was an idea that seemed like something out of Star Trek – that you could have something in your pocket that you would use to conduct your business, watch TV or a film, speak to someone in China and more, all with one device.

Technology is changing the way we do business every single day, and we live in an age of rapid technological change.

Adapting to that change is really important. When you're looking at growth and new avenues, technology should always be taken into account.

Here is a statistic to finish this chapter on, before you get out that pen and fill in a PEST analysis.

In the decade 2010 – 2020 – technology developed at the same rate as it had over the previous forty years.

In March 2020 – September 2020 – technology and its use developed in seven months faster than the rate it did over the past ten years.

Think about that figure, in seven months, forty years of technological was achieved.....

What's next for your business?

Chapter Nine
Key Partners

Key partners are really important element to any business, because they are what will help you to expand and grow.

No business is an island that operates on its own.

Goal Setting

If you have a goal or plan from a growth perspective, write down what it is.

Write down what you'll do in the next three months – what are you looking to achieve and what do you think you will achieve?

The reason for writing it down is because you're much more likely to achieve it and reach your goal rather than by just having it in your head.

You're less likely to go off track.

Am I repeating myself?

Have I said this in other parts of the book?

Good.

I meant to, that's just how important this is.

Key Partners

Who are your current key business partners?

By key partners, we mean people who can help you advance your business in any kind of fashion.

For example, I know a female-owned and led business whose key partner is not within the company or a supplier, but her childminder.

Without the childminder, she wouldn't be able to go to work each day, because she has two children and is solely responsible for their care.

The childminder gives her the space to run her business. In terms of business growth, it also allows her the flexibility to know that her childcare is taken care of.

Business key partners don't just have to be the people who you think are directly related to your company. They can be the people who facilitate your working life.

Key Suppliers

Who are your key suppliers and why?

If you have a product that you manufacture, then you know that there are component and supplier parts to take that forward.

However, if you're a service-based business, who could your key suppliers be? It could be your stationery supplier, or the person who gives you bags for your retail business.

What do You get From Them?

What do you get from your partners and suppliers that's a resource you can use?

Do you get advice?

Do you have people you can talk to?

These are the key resources that may not be the obvious things, like stationery, that they bring to your business.

Now you've identified your partners and suppliers, revisit your goal plan.

Think about your key partners and suppliers, the resources you get from them, and apply that directly to how you'll reach your growth goal at the end of the three months.

My Developers

First list all of your developers.

Then rate each developer on a scale of 1-5 based on the assistance they provide to you or your business growth.

1	2	3	4	5
Never	Rarely	Sometimes	Often	Always

Developer Name	Helps me take action	Helps me advance my goals	Provides personal support	Is a role model for me
Total				

Now work out where your lowest mark is. This is the area to first work on when looking to build your development network.

Chapter Ten
Revenue Growth
Strategies & Pricing

When we have developed our key partners and developers and used our growth plan to identify the areas we need to work upon, it really is time to revisit our revenue growth strategies.

Revenue growth strategies are the way we can work out which of our customers we should be looking at building our business with.

This is a little bit like when we identified with our key partners we are looking to establish more information about how we can utilise our new and existing customer base to help us to grow.

Customers – New and Existing

Which customers are the best for us to approach?

Do we always have to be approaching new customers?

I did some research on where our time should be spent when we are personally looking at revenue growth.

Just to be clear, revenue growth is the amount of money that comes into a business to help it grow.

The amount of growth that you'll get from approaching a new customer with a new product or service is only 3%.

If you spend a lot of time trying to attract new customers to new products and services, 3% is the maximum increase in sales you'll get.

This is a very small return for a lot of work. However, if you took a new customer and tried to sell them an existing product, one you sold every day, the revenue growth increases to 10%.

Why You Should Sell More to Existing Customers

What gets more interesting is if you take an existing customer and sell them an existing product or service, revenue would increase by 15%.

By having a relationship with an existing customer already, selling them more of your existing offerings means you will get a revenue increase.

You may say, "But those are already our customers, already using our offering."

What's interesting is that, most research has shown that 80% of every business' revenue comes from 20% of their clients.

So, if we took 100 clients, only 20 of them would account for 80% of the revenue.

That leaves 80 of them, essentially, to target. The 80/20 rule is a really good way of growing your business.

More importantly, if you took an existing customer and gave them a new product, it's up to a 25% increase in revenue.

Surely, mathematically, giving existing customers new products, when they already know, like, and trust you, makes sense.

By using that customer and offering a new product or service, you can increase revenue up to 25%.

It's a no-brainer!

I'm not saying don't look for new customers or offerings, because you should be doing those things, but not to the detriment of serving existing customers with new products, because that's where the revenue will come from.

Revenue Growth Strategies

Products

	Existing	New
Customers		
New		
Existing		

In the table write down in each box the corresponding name of your customer base.

So for example are the existing customers buying new products?

They would be listed in the bottom right hand corner box

And so on.

When you have listed all of your customers for at least the next month, have a look and see which of the boxes are filled most.

Now if the box that says existing and new is not the most filled in, we have something to work on.

We have identified that you are not utilising your client base and selling enough new products to the base you already have.

How are we going to alter that?

Remember the differentiation task? These two tasks work together very well.

Get out that pen! You have some work to do!

Pricing

No matter how long people have been in business, pricing is always something that they need help with.

How and why you choose prices and the reason behind a pricing strategy are always difficult for people.

The Four Main Areas of Pricing

The interesting thing about pricing is that it's not always about cost.

Sometimes it's about feelings, desires and marketing.

When we think about pricing, we need to consider what's happening in our marketplace.

1. Comparison

What is actually happening with similar products or services to yours?

From a comparison point of view, can we rank our offerings into categories? Is there a premium product or service, and is your business or offering comparable to that?

Is there a cheaper version or a race to the bottom?

Are you marketing your business on price alone?

If you do, it's always going to be difficult to move up in the price range from there.

Conversely, are you a middle of the road product?

These are marketing issues rather than pricing issues. You're thinking about where you sit in the market; and your price will reflect that.

It's nothing to do with cost, margins or value, it's all to do with the marketing message you're giving.

In order to do a comparison, have you done your research? Have you identified where those similar markets are?

2. Cost and Margin

This is the correct way to price something.

What is the actual cost for you to produce that product or service? When we think about cost, we think about every element of cost.

Is there a cost for marketing, time or materials?

Only by identifying all of those things and adding them together can you find the true cost to you, your business and your offering.

Once you've identified the cost, what is the profit margin that you would like to make? Is it 1%, so that for everything you sell or make you make 1% margin, or is it 150% or 200%?

This then goes back to the price comparison.

In your marketplace, can you provide a margin of 150%, 200% or 50%?

As a rule of thumb, margins are around 55% to 70%. Keeping this in mind, go back through your cost and margin and work out if you're pricing your product or service correctly.

And if you are not, is there a reason you have a very low margin?

Is it to keep your price lower than a competitor?

Is it a marketing decision rather than a pricing decision?

Was it unintentional?

3. Value to Customer

What is the value to the customer that you provide?

Is it something intrinsic that your customer can't do without?

Can you charge a premium price, because without you, your customer would be desperate and unable to move forwards?

This is often marketing-based.

Remember when we did the benefits in a previous chapter, could that be some help to you here when you are trying to establish a value.

4. Make it up

Completely make your prices up!

Try a really high price, and if somebody buys your product or service at your high price, that's wonderful.

If not, you can always reduce the price, but making it up is worth a go as long as you know the actual cost of producing that product or service. Over the years I can't tell you how many businesses I have worked with who have a priced a product without costing out the whole thing and realising all too late they were making a loss each time they provided that product or service.

Pricing is not always about cost, so bear that in mind. As long as you've worked out your basic costs to provide the product or service, everything else is around marketing.

Don't get hung up on the fact that you're premium, cheap or middle. By knowing your true cost and understanding marketing, you can identify where your price points should be for your business, product or service.

Chapter Eleven
Business Process Model & Closing The Sale

What is a Business Process Model?

It's the functionality of the way that you do business.

For example, take a look at McDonald's.

Their business process model is what they operate on around the world. If we look at the hamburger, I can guarantee the burger you buy from McDonald's in London is the same as the one you buy in Paris, Berlin, Moscow and America.

They have the same size bun, burger and gherkin and use the same amount of sauce, mustard and onion.

They have a process which every employee knows.

For example, the bottom of the bun will slide along, the beef goes in, two squirts of tomato sauce and one of mustard.

Then, two gherkins are added – but not on top of each other – followed by three scoops of onion and the lid.

The hamburger is wrapped and out for service. It's the same process all the way through, and each product McDonald's sells in every restaurant around the world is created in exactly the same way.

Why Do You Need a Business Process Model?

The most successful businesses identify what their business process is.

It doesn't matter whether you're in the food, retail or service industry, every one of us can do a business process model.

For example, in my day job, I deliver training.

We have a business process we follow every time we write a new training course, and the first step is doing the research for the course.

Number two is identifying the target customer, then developing and practising the course, then finding someone who wants to pay for it.

We have a process now that's set through a number of years' experience.

Take a look at your business and your current processes, and think about. If you fell into a hole tomorrow, is there a business process you could create for someone to follow and understand your business?

A third example is Subway.

You go into a shop and buy a six inch or foot long baguette and you know where you are along the row.

You get three slices of ham and unlimited vegetables, and the process for how to make and wrap sandwiches is there for the staff to follow.

It's like a production line, and you need to think of your business as such.

Take some time to sit down and think about what are the business processes that go into making your business, your business.

There won't just be one process; there may be five processes, 10 or 15, depending on what your business is, but you should be able to identify them.

Why is that important?

Well, it's important to develop the processes because that's how you grow.

Once you know what they are, you can either replicate them or have somebody else come in and take them over so you can go off and concentrate on something else.

The business process model is the most important and interesting part of your business.

It's interesting because you get to review everything that's happening within your business on a daily, weekly, monthly or annual basis.

By knowing those things, you can build and grow your company and develop over time.

Business Process Model

Actions	Responsibilities	Who/Roles

You can use the Business Process Model sheet to remind you of the things you would like to design, but as good as this sheet is, I always find having a huge pile of Post-It Notes is a good way of working out each step of the process.

List down each step of the process and include all of the processes of your business.

Think about the areas such as sales, payments, key partners, products, online and invoicing.

Suddenly you can see how important the business process model becomes.

Once this is in place we can start to identify the areas to grow and build upon.

If you have been reading the book in a linear fashion, think about the chapter on ideas generation. How can we use the things we learnt from that chapter to introduce new processes, new ideas and improve upon the things in existence?

The business process model is the thing that is the living, breathing example of your business and all it can be.

Get out that pen and those sticky notes and find three areas of improvement today.

Can you find more than three?

Note them down, and start to plan!

Closing the Sale

Everybody admits that the one thing they worry about is how to get more sales.

Sometimes, the problem isn't 'how do we get more sales', but 'how do we close more sales', or potential sales we have.

Answer this: How many potential customers do you have each week, month or year (depending on your business) that walk away without actually buying your product or service?

It's an important question to know the answer to, because to get that person or business into a conversation is really hard work.

Once you've got them there, once you understand the fundamentals of turning them into a customer, you'll have a customer for life.

The Five Elements Which Prevent Closing a Sale

Work through each of these elements, thinking about the last potential customer you dealt with. Were any of them the reason why they didn't become a customer?

1. No Money

This is true a small percentage of the time, but money is never a factor in closing a sale.

Money coupled with some of the other factors could be why you don't close the sale, but on its own it's not a factor.

2. No Time

"I'm rushed, I don't have time to find out more about this or add it into my day."

No time is an excuse! Somebody who's interested will find the time.

My example on this is, if you've spoken to somebody for 10 minutes and they walk on and say, "I haven't got the time to listen", then you haven't piqued their interest or given them what they need.

When we talk about brand values, we talk about what the things are that people see, makes them feel better and makes them want to use your business or service.

This is where time comes in, so try to overcome this excuse.

3. No Need

"I've seen this, you've shown me it, but I've got no need for it."

Again, from a sales perspective and for closing the sale, your job is to show that potential customer why they should buy your product or service and why they should have that need and be excited about it.

4. No Urgency

If they think they can get it from you at any time, and they can come back to you in six or 12 months or even three years, there's no urgency there.

You need to be aware of urgency, but you also need to create it.

The first three elements together combine to create the fourth. Creating an urgency and a demand for your product or service is really important to help you close the deal.

5. No Trust

This is the killer for any sale.

If the potential customer does not trust what you're saying, that your product or service is good, or it's not the thing they need in their lives, then they will not buy from you, regardless if none of the other elements apply.

Trust and relationship building are the key to any sale, and especially to closing it. You must work on some of those trust words. To close a sale, you need to create an environment where none of these five elements are an issue.

How To Close A Sale

Review your last ten potential sales. Answer the following to illustrate which parts of your sales process are working and which are not. Be honest, it will help you to put together a more successful sales pitch, either written or verbal.

1. Money - did the sale fall down on cost? Why?

_____

_____

_____

2. Time - did the customer not have the time to invest to listen to why the product/service was right for them?

_____

_____

_____

3. Need - What's the phrase you will use to convince people to buy your product or service?

_____

_____

_____

4. Urgency - How will you create a sense of urgency for people to buy your product or your service. What words will you use?

_____

_____

_____

5. Trust - How do you build trust in you, your product or your service. What are the 3 words you will use to help build trust?

1. _____

2. _____

3. _____

Chapter Twelve
Tell The Truth

Let's be truthful about your business — did you start it because you had to?

Have you fallen out of love with it?

The questions I'll ask because no one else will.

It's quite common that someone who's started a business or is well along the road to growth finds that they're not as excited, motivated or passionate about the business that they started.

They may feel trapped and not sure how to get out of it.

It is not an impossible or difficult situation to get out of, but what is difficult is recognising and noticing that you've trapped yourself.

Here are some ideas to get yourself out of that situation, but also how you can improve it.

Five Key Areas

1. What did You Love About Your Business?

Identify what is was you loved when you started your business. What were the things that made you feel passionate? What gave you that feeling where you jumped out of bed and thought, "I really need to work in my business. I'm so excited about it!"

By identifying them, you can recognise where the changes have happened and where things are going wrong.

2. What are You Great at?

Identify what you're great at and blow your own trumpet. Say to yourself, "These are the things that I'm the best in the world at doing, and nobody else can do them as well as me."

Those are the things that give you confidence, reinvigorate you and make you feel better about life.

3. What Does Your World Need?

Identify what your world needs from you.

Are you just feeling unhappy in your business because you've got lots of things going on in your life?

Are there other things surrounding your business that are affecting your desire and passion and how you want to move with things?

Is it not your business that's making you unhappy, but the rest of your world and what you're surrounded by?

Take some time to do a life audit to see if there's something happening personally that could affect what's happening professionally?

4. Make a List

What are the things that people value and pay you for?

What are the things that people get inspired by you for?

Why do they pay you for your product or service?

Why do they pay for your product/service and why do they pay your company anything at all?

What makes them passionate about it and become an advocate?

5. How Much Time do You Waste?

This may seem like an odd question, but so many business owners are unhappy because they feel that they're trapped with not much time.

They think that they have too much to do and too little time, but that isn't actually the issue.

In fact, the issue is that they waste too much time, so the tasks that they have to do become a chore and feel difficult.

Asking yourself these questions will make you feel better about your business, but you may also come to a decision.

It may be a realisation that the business isn't actually for you, which is not a problem either.

However, in order to make a decision and to move forward, you need to review what's gone on before. To find your mojo, maybe you need to review the past that made you lose it in the first place.

Chapter Thirteen
Unlucky For Some

Why oh why did I finish this my first book on chapter thirteen.

Does it mean anything?

Will it mean that people won't buy it?

Or will it mean that I'll have to finish the book on some truths to counteract the unlucky 13 number?

I'll go with the truths.

I've read it in so many books about how they were a labour of love to write.

This wasn't.

Don't get me wrong, I love the book now it's written and I am very proud of its content, but the writing part of it was just a labour.

The second, more difficult book is planned, but this was a labour.

It's been all over the world with me, sitting in my bag waiting to be finished.

Why has it been such a labour? Let me tell you. I love to impart this knowledge.

This knowledge that I know will change people's businesses and their lives.

I want to impart it to as many business owners as possible and I want them to take it and adopt it and to do it.

Then I want them to write to me and to tell me the difference it has made to their business and their lives.

So why has it been so difficult to write it?

Here's the thing.

I impart this knowledge all of the time, in person, in training, in key notes and in all sorts of verbal ways.

Writing it down was a struggle. I wanted it to reflect my voice and sound like me.

No holding back, no gloss, just the truthful way of how to grow your business.

Will it work. Yes. How do I know?

Well, I have presented and taught this method now for over three years and I have demonstrable outcomes to prove it.

In my own business and in others.

So now I want you to prove me wrong.

I want you to get that pen out, to do every task we have demonstrated and written about and then put them into action.

You will make a difference, I promise you.

You will see your business grow.

You will feel more in charge of your destiny.

Finally, you will have a plan written down to stick to.

Then you are going to join the other business owners as part of my Facebook group.

In Cahoots with Phil.

And share your wins and your losses and the things that have and haven't worked for you and they will support you at every turn.

www.facebook.com/groups/ incahootswithphil/

I also want you to talk to me in the group, to share your stories and I want to give you more and more training based around the things I am learning from In Cahoots.

If you have enjoyed the book and you would like to undertake the In Cahoots training online you can find it here:

www.enterprisemadesimple.co.uk

Where you can also find lots of my other training sessions and keynotes, blogs etc for you to download and take part in.

I'm glad I wrote the book by the way, I feel proud of it.

But I like to deliver this stuff in person most.

In fact I would go as far as to say it's the thing I do best - coaching and training.

If you want some one to one coaching, I can oblige, check out the website.

Thank you for buying this book, I really appreciate it.

NOW

Get out that pen.

Start to implement the lessons.

Keep a record and all of the data on how much you have grown.

I can't wait to watch you fly.

Thank you

P Teasdale

A System To Grow, Scale & Sustain Your Business

In Cahoots
The Programme